DO THIS IN REMEMBRANCE

An Introduction to the Sacraments

WORKBOOK

TAN Books
Gastonia, North Carolina

Do This in Remembrance: An Introduction to the Sacraments Workbook © 2021 TAN Books

All rights reserved. With the exception of short excerpts used in critical review, no part of this work may be reproduced, transmitted, or stored in any form whatsoever, without the prior written permission of the publisher.

Unless otherwise noted, Scripture quotations are from the Revised Standard Version of the Bible—Second Catholic Edition (Ignatius Edition), copyright © 2006 National Council of the Churches of Christ in the United States of America. Used by permission. All rights reserved.

Compiled by Melissa Girard

Series design by Margaret Ryland

Cover and layout by Caroline Green

Cover image: *The Last Supper* (c. 1562), Juan de Juanes, Museo del Prado, Madrid, Spain

ISBN: 978-1-5051-1943-5

Published in the United States by
TAN Books
PO Box 269
Gastonia, NC 28053
www.TANBooks.com

Printed in the United States of America

DO THIS IN REMEMBRANCE

An Introduction to the Sacraments

WORKBOOK

Contents

A Note to Instructors vii

PART I: THE SACRAMENTAL ECONOMY
Chapter 1: Definition of Sacrament 3
Chapter 2: Redemption Is Mediated Through the Sacraments. 6

PART II: BAPTISM
Chapter 1: Understanding the Sacrament. 13
Chapter 2: Living the Sacrament 17

PART III: CONFIRMATION
Chapter 1: Understanding the Sacrament. 23
Chapter 2: Living the Sacrament 26

PART IV: THE EUCHARIST
Chapter 1: Understanding the Sacrament. 33
Chapter 2: Living the Sacrament 36

PART V: PENANCE AND RECONCILIATION
Chapter 1: Understanding the Sacrament. 43
Chapter 2: Living the Sacrament 47

PART VI: ANOINTING OF THE SICK
Chapter 1: Understanding the Sacrament. 53
Chapter 2: Living the Sacrament 57

PART VII: HOLY ORDERS
Chapter 1: Understanding the Sacrament. 63
Chapter 2: Living the Sacrament 66

PART VIII: HOLY MATRIMONY
Chapter 1: Understanding the Sacrament 71
Chapter 2: Living the Sacrament 75

Final Exam 78

Answer Key 81

A Note to Instructors

As Pope St. John Paul II made clear in his apostolic exhortation *Catechesi Tradendae*, "The definitive aim of catechesis is to put people not only in touch but in communion, in intimacy, with Jesus Christ."

The *Formed in Christ* series seeks to fulfill this call, fostering intimacy with Christ through its dynamic content.

Rather than presenting religion as any other subject to be mastered, our series editors have designed each text to plumb the bottomless genius of Catholicism found in centuries of theologians, saints, councils, and papal teachings.

The six volumes in *Formed in Christ* cover every point in the USCCB's guidelines for high school catechesis.

Do This in Remembrance provides an examination of the sacramental nature of the Church and makes clear Christ's presence and activity in the sacraments of initiation (Baptism, Confirmation, Eucharist) and the sacraments at the service of Communion (Holy Matrimony, Holy Orders). It provides the scriptural basis and historic development of the sacraments, sheds light on how they are celebrated, and presents the effects they have in the life of the believer.

This supplemental workbook is designed to provide instructors with test material and direction for enhancing students' grasp of the material.

For each chapter, the following components are included:

Memory Verse

Appealing not only to the head but also the heart, a suitable memory verse, chosen for its relation to the chapter's content, is suggested to help the student with his or her prayer life. Throughout the week, have your student attempt to recite this verse from memory.

Key Terms

A list of key terms from the chapter is included. Students are encouraged to write down some notes about these terms (either here in the workbook or in a separate notebook), using not only the text but the *Catechism of the Catholic Church* and a good Catholic dictionary as well. This will not only prepare students for testing but deepen their understanding of the content.

Questions for Review
Taken directly from the student text, the Questions for Review, provided in "short answer" format, ensure comprehension of the material. Answers are provided in the back.

Quiz
For each chapter, ten questions are provided for testing. Multiple Choice, True or False, and Fill-in-the-Blank quizzes vary throughout the workbook. Answers are provided in the back.

Questions for Discussion
Dialogue between students and instructors is essential. Not only will the Questions for Discussion (included both here and in the student text), provide another opportunity for reinforcing the material, but the questions are specifically designed to prompt students to reflect on their own faith experience. While discussion between students and instructors is highly recommended, the Questions for Discussion can also be used as prompts for personal writing exercises. Since these are more for personal reflection, no answers are provided.

Essay Topics and/or Further Study
The *Formed in Christ* series is designed to expose students to Church documents and the writings of theologians from all stages of Church history. But these selected readings are just the beginning of Catholic thought that students can discover. The Essay Topics and/or Further Study suggestions encourage students to dig deeper into the wealth of Catholic teaching through independent study. A mix of personal, subjective prompts and research topics, these suggestions will enable your student to learn more about his or her Catholic faith. Grading is left up to the instructor's discretion.

Final Exam
In the back, you will find a final exam that aggregates all the most important content. This provides a barometer for how well your student absorbed the material. It consists of matching and short answer. Answers are provided in the back.

Part I

The Sacramental Economy

Part I: Chapter 1

Definition of Sacrament

Memory Verse

> Let what you heard from the beginning abide in you. If what you heard from the beginning abides in you, then you will abide in the Son and in the Father.
>
> —1 John 2:24

Key Terms

Sacrament

Holy Spirit

St. Augustine

Actual grace

Habitual grace

Sanctifying grace

Signs

Salvation

Questions for Review

1. What was the meaning of the word *sacramentum* in the ancient Roman world?

2. What is the difference between the sacraments of the Church and the customs of Roman soldiers?

3. What is sanctifying grace?

4. How does the Church define "sacrament"?

5. Why do we call the Church "the universal sacrament of salvation"?

Quiz

True/False

1. ____ *Sacramentum* is a Latin legal term and can refer to a military oath.
2. ____ Though the sacraments have certain similarities to secular rites of passage, the power of the Magisterium is what makes the sacraments different.
3. ____ Habitual grace is the grace that God gives us that enables us to act.
4. ____ The strengthening grace God gives us is called habitual grace.
5. ____ Sanctifying grace is a supernatural disposition but not a habitual gift.
6. ____ Sacraments are transformative words of God that he gave to human persons to speak.
7. ____ The sacraments are efficacious signs that also make the thing they point to happen.
8. ____ Properly speaking, the Church is a sacrament.
9. ____ St. Augustine told us that in the early Church, outsiders would marvel at the example of Christians.

10. ___ The Church is called the universal sacrament of salvation because it points to the sacraments while also fulfilling them.

Questions for Discussion

1. How important are the sacraments in your life right now? What are you looking forward to learning about the sacraments as you study them with the aid of this book?

2. Have you ever felt particularly close to God after receiving a sacrament? If so, describe your experience. If not, or if you have not yet received any sacraments, have you ever known anyone who did feel this way?

Essay Topics / Further Study

1. In this chapter, we read about the military oaths that Roman soldiers took. Find a modern example of a rite of initiation. How is it similar to the sacraments? How is it different?

2. Interview a parent, grandparent, or family friend about a time when they have experienced the power of the Holy Spirit through the sacraments.

3. With the help of your Catechism and a Catholic dictionary, write an essay defining and explaining actual, habitual, and sanctifying grace.

4. Compare a "sign" or "ceremony" in the secular world to one of the sacraments. How is it the same? How is it different?

5. Reflect on Tertullian's statement about the love of the early Christians. Do you think Catholics today give the same witness to the world? Give as many examples as you can find.

Part I: Chapter 2

Redemption Is Mediated Through the Sacraments

Memory Verse

> In the beginning was the Word, and the Word was with God, and the Word was God. He was in the beginning with God. All things came into being through him, and without him not one thing came into being. What has come into being in him was life, and the life was the light of all people. The light shines in the darkness, and the darkness did not overcome it.
>
> —John 1:1–5

Key terms

Signs

Causes

Primary cause

Instrumental cause

Covenants

Prefigure

Holy Spirit

Sacraments of initiation

Sacraments of healing

Sacraments at the service of Communion

Questions for Review

1. What is the difference between a primary cause and an instrumental cause (in regards to the administering of a sacrament)?

2. How did God prepare humanity for a sacramental relationship with himself in the Old Testament?

3. What is the difference between the covenantal signs in the Old Testament and the sacraments of the New Testament?

4. What happened to the Old Testament signs when Jesus came?

5. Into what three categories does the Church typically divide the sacraments?

Quiz

1. The sacraments only give us the Holy Spirit because they are backed by _____.

2. The object or person who initiates an action is called a _____.

3. The tool through which an action is done is called an _____.

4. God prepared us for a sacramental relationship with him through a series of _____ in the Old Testament.

5. The signs of the Old Testament were not true _____.

6. St. Paul said that the signs of the Old Testament _____ the sacraments of the Church.

7. When Jesus came, the Old Testament signs _____.

8. Jesus commanded _____ to bring the Holy Spirit to others through the sacraments.

9. Reconciliation is considered a sacrament _____.

10. Holy Orders is considered a sacrament at the service of _____.

Questions for Discussion

1. Has there ever been a time when God worked through you to do good to another? Describe what that felt like.

2. Oftentimes we have to wait for God's best gifts in our lives. Can you think of a time when you had to wait to receive something good? How did God prepare your heart to receive it while you were waiting?

Essay Topics / Further Study

1. In this chapter's selected reading from the Catechism, we read about the visible and spiritual aspects of the Church. Explain how the Church can simultaneously be a "society structured with hierarchical organs and the mystical body of Christ," "the visible society and spiritual community," and "the earthly Church and the Church endowed with heavenly riches." Give examples to illustrate each of these seeming paradoxes.

2. Find both Old Testament and New Testament examples of where God's words made something happen.

3. Choose one of the Old Testament covenants to define and explain. Which aspects of the seven sacraments does it prefigure, if any?

4. Although the covenants of the Old Testament were not sacraments properly speaking, why was it important for God's people to be faithful to them?

5. Jesus gave the Holy Spirit to the apostles and commanded them to share the Holy Spirit through the Church and the sacraments. Where do you find evidence for this in the Church today?

Part II

BAPTISM

Part II: Chapter 1

Understanding the Sacrament

Memory Verse

> And when Jesus had been baptized, just as he came up from the water, suddenly the heavens were opened to him and he saw the Spirit of God descending like a dove and alighting on him. And a voice from heaven said, "This is my Son, the Beloved, with whom I am well pleased."
>
> —Matthew 3:16–17

Key Terms

Protoevangelium

Deicide

Sin

Repentance

Water

Baptism

Catechumenate

Christian initiation

Limbo

Baptism of blood

Baptism of desire

Questions for Review

1. Before the Fall, what could Adam and Eve learn from water about their relationship with God?

2. After the Fall, how did God use water to bring about purification from sin? Give two examples.

3. Why was Jesus baptized?

4. Is Baptism necessary for salvation?

5. What is a Baptism of desire? What is a Baptism of blood?

Quiz

1. The promise of a savior that is issued immediately after the first sin is called:
   A. the Gospel.
   B. the Protoevangelium.
   C. the Kerygma.

2. The act of killing God is called:
   A. Deicide.
   B. Theicide.
   C. Homicide.

3. Jesus's baptism reflects a redeemed relationship with:
    A. water.
    B. God the Father.
    C. humanity.

4. We can be certain that:
    A. everyone who has been baptized will obtain heaven.
    B. those who have not been baptized will receive the grace of salvation.
    C. everyone needs to be baptized.

5. In the early Church, the process of Christian initiation leading to Baptism was:
    A. secretive.
    B. short.
    C. lengthy.

6. _____ are those preparing to be received into the Church.
    A. Protoevangelists
    B. Catechumens
    C. Sponsors

7. Baptism of desire:
    A. is not a Baptism, properly speaking.
    B. can occur when someone was uncertain if they desired Baptism.
    C. would require that one delayed or failed to request Baptism.

8. The Church believes that God would not refuse to offer baptismal grace to someone who had unwavering faith and were killed out of hatred for faith in Christ. This is referred to as:
    A. baptism of desire.
    B. baptism of fire.
    C. baptism of blood.

9. _____ is understood as a place where unbaptized babies are separated from the vision of God but do not suffer from any torments.
    A. Purgatory
    B. Limbo
    C. Sheol

10. The Church entrusts the unbaptized to:
    A. fate.
    B. God's justice.
    C. God's mercy.

Questions for Discussion

1. How can the baptism of Jesus help us think about the relationship that God wants to have with us in our own baptism?

2. Why do some people have a hard time with the idea that Baptism is necessary for salvation? How can you best respond?

Essay Topics / Further Study

1. Find a concordance online and search for the term "water." Make a list of a dozen references to water in both the Old Testament and the New. In light of this chapter, what makes the examples that you have chosen significant?

2. Reflect on the story of the parting of the Red Sea. What elements of the story are similar to our relationship with sin and God's grace? In what way does this story help you better understand the need for Baptism?

3. Write about a scenario in which baptism by desire could take place.

4. Write about a scenario in which baptism by blood could take place.

5. Interview someone you know who has gone through the process of RCIA. What was it like for them? What do they remember about the moment of their baptism?

Part II: Chapter 2

Living the Sacrament

Memory Verse

> May you be strengthened with all power, according to his glorious might, for all endurance and patience with joy, giving thanks to the Father, who has qualified us to share in the inheritance of the saints in light. He has delivered us from the dominion of darkness and transferred us to the kingdom of his beloved Son, in whom we have redemption, the forgiveness of sins.
>
> —Colossians 1:11–14

Key Terms

Trinitarian formula

Original sin

Personal sin

Concupiscence

Mortal sin

Venial sin

Sanctifying grace

Character

Questions for Review

1. What are the necessary words that must be spoken in Baptism?

2. Who ordinarily administers the sacrament? Are there any exceptions to this?

3. What types of sins are forgiven in Baptism?

4. What "new beginnings" does Baptism mark?

5. What do we call the spiritual mark Baptism leaves on us? Can that mark ever be taken away?

Quiz

True/False

1. ____ The Trinitarian formula is required for Baptism.
2. ____ The rite of Baptism includes one or more exorcisms.
3. ____ The newly baptized are given one gift: a white garment.
4. ____ Parents do not have a right to choose Baptism for their children.
5. ____ Original sin is the first sin a person commits.
6. ____ Concupiscence is the inclination to sin.
7. ____ Venial sin can be committed when we are inculpably ignorant that we are doing so.
8. ____ Baptism marks the beginning of the presence of actual grace.
9. ____ Being a member of the Church requires unity, cooperation, contribution, and coordination.
10. ____ The spiritual mark imparted to us through Baptism is called mystagogy.

Questions for Discussion

1. Do you remember your baptism day? If so, what was special about if? If not, or if you have not yet been baptized, have you been to someone else's baptism? What seemed special about it?

2. What are some ways you can call upon the graces you received on your baptism day? If you have not already been baptized, why do you think the Church urges people to do this?

Essay Topics / Further Study

1. Write about a scenario in which someone who is not baptized could baptize another person.

2. Find an example from Scripture where anointing with sacred chrism takes place. How does it relate to the anointing with oil that takes place in Baptism?

3. Write a persuasive essay on the importance of parents choosing Baptism for their children. Why is it important to baptize a child as soon as possible versus letting them make their own decision when they come to the age of reason?

4. Research mortal sin and venial sin. What does the Church teach about each? Why is it important to be free of both?

5. What reminders do we have in the Church of our baptism? List as many you can think of.

Part III

Confirmation

Part III: Chapter 1

Understanding the Sacrament

Memory Verse

> It is not for you to know times or seasons which the Father has fixed by his own authority. But you shall receive power when the Holy Spirit has come upon you; and you shall be my witnesses in Jerusalem and in all Judea and Samar′ia and to the end of the earth.
>
> —Acts 1:7–8

Key Terms

Oil

Priests

Prophet

King

Messiah

Christos

Pentecost

Chrismation

Questions for Review

1. In the ancient world, what did oil symbolize?

2. In the Old Testament, what were the three categories of people anointed by oil and why were they anointed?

3. Who was anointed in the Gospels?

4. What is received in Confirmation?

5. For what do the gifts we receive in Confirmation prepare us?

Quiz

1. In a sense, oil brings perfection to _____.

2. The use of oil as a sign of perfection is always accompanied by a sign of _____.

3. The olive leaf carried by a dove after the Great Flood symbolizes _____, health, and beauty.

4. _____ were anointed to govern and assist the Israelites in their obedience to God through prayer.

PART III: CHAPTER 1
UNDERSTANDING THE SACRAMENT

5. _____ were anointed to speak the words of God to the Israelites.

6. _____ were anointed to offer sacrifice on behalf of Israel.

7. In Hebrew, *Mashiach* means Messiah, or _____.

8. The Greek word that is a direct translation of the Hebrew word for Messiah is _____.

9. In the _____, there was a tendency to emphasize that Confirmation raises us up to spiritual maturity.

10. In the _____, there was a tendency to emphasize that Confirmation is a completion of Baptism.

Questions for Discussion

1. Why do you think Christians need special graces to give witness to Jesus in the world? What can make giving this witness difficult?

2. Describe a situation you have been in where it was difficult to follow Jesus or be a good witness to him. What happened? How can asking the Holy Spirit for help strengthen you to face similar situations in the future?

Essay Topics / Further Study

1. The uses of oil in the ancient world are fascinating. Study why oil was important to the ancient Israelites. Are there any celebrations in particular where oil is used?

2. Choose one Old Testament priest who demonstrates the gifts of the Holy Spirit. How does that priest prefigure the priesthood of Christ?

3. Choose one Old Testament prophet who demonstrates the gifts of the Holy Spirit. How does that prophet prefigure the prophecy of Christ?

4. Choose one Old Testament king who demonstrates the gifts of the Holy Spirit. How does that king prefigure the kingship of Christ?

Part III: Chapter 2

Living the Sacrament

Memory Verse

> The Spirit of the Lord shall rest on him,
>   the spirit of wisdom and understanding,
>   the spirit of counsel and might,
>   the spirit of knowledge and the fear of the Lord.

—Isaiah 11:2

Key Terms

Chrism

Age of discretion

Chrism Mass

Gifts of the Holy Spirit

Fruits of the Holy Spirit

Seal

Lectio divina

Liturgy of the Hours

Questions for Review

1. What are the essential words that must be spoken in the sacrament of Confirmation?

2. Who is the original minister of Confirmation? Who else can administer the sacrament?

3. Is Confirmation necessary for salvation? Why or why not?

4. Name three effects of Confirmation.

5. What can affect the extent to which we benefit from the graces of Confirmation?

Quiz

1. "Be sealed with the Gifts of the Holy Spirit" are the words used at the:
    A. Chrism Mass.
    B. Easter Vigil.
    C. central moment of Confirmation.

2. The original minister of the sacrament of Confirmation is:
    A. Peter.
    B. the bishop.
    C. Jesus.

3. Priests must use _____ consecrated by a bishop for Confirmation.
    A. chrism
    B. hands
    C. candles

4. In the Latin Rite, children are typically confirmed at:
   A. Baptism.
   B. First Communion.
   C. the age of discretion.

5. Confirmation is not necessary for:
   A. salvation.
   B. receiving Holy Orders.
   C. holiness.

6. Any priest can confer the sacrament of Confirmation on the baptized in:
   A. the case of desire.
   B. the season of Easter.
   C. the danger of death.

7. Those being confirmed need to seek _____ to help shepherd them through the sacrament.
   A. godparents
   B. sponsors
   C. guardians

8. The signs and ceremonies of Confirmation continue on and reflect:
   A. Baptism.
   B. the Easter Vigil.
   C. the Mass.

9. Fortitude, knowledge, and piety are examples of:
   A. the fruits of the Spirit.
   B. the gifts of the Spirit.
   C. the signs of the Spirit.

10. Joy, peace, and kindness are examples of:
    A. the fruits of the Spirit.
    B. the gifts of the Spirit.
    C. the signs of the Spirit.

Questions for Discussion

1. Do you remember your Confirmation? If so, what was special about the day? If not, or if you have not yet been confirmed, have you ever attended someone's Confirmation? What seemed interesting about the celebration?

2. Do you ever pray to the Holy Spirit? Why or why not? How could this help you grow stronger in your faith? How else could you strengthen your relationship with the Holy Spirit?

PART III: CHAPTER 2
LIVING THE SACRAMENT

Essay Topic / Further Study

1. What are the requirements and preparation needed for receiving the sacrament of Confirmation?

2. The sacrament of Confirmation contributes to our spiritual maturity. Find a saint who, at a very young age, demonstrated spiritual maturity. What can they teach you about following Jesus?

3. What are some of the ways that you can identify the work of the Holy Spirit in someone's life? Use Scripture and the lives of the saints to provide examples.

4. With the help of your Catechism or a Catholic dictionary, define each of the gifts of the Holy Spirit and provide a real world example of that gift showing itself.

5. Choose one of the fruits of the Holy Spirit to study further. Provide examples of when you've witnessed others demonstrate this fruit. Have you experienced this fruit of the Spirit in your own life?

Part IV

The Eucharist

Part IV: Chapter 1

Understanding the Sacrament

Memory Verse

> I am the bread of life. Your ancestors ate the manna in the wilderness, and they died. This is the bread that comes down from heaven, so that one may eat of it and not die. I am the living bread that came down from heaven. Whoever eats of this bread will live forever; and the bread that I will give for the life of the world is my flesh.
>
> —John 6:48–51

Key Terms

Sacrifice

Feeding of the Five Thousand

Bread of Life Discourse

Passover

Remembrance

Accidents

Substance

Transubstantiation

Questions for Review

1. What is the fundamental element of a sacrifice?

2. What could the sacrifices of the Old Testament not accomplish? What could they accomplish?

3. In what three ways did Jesus promise to fulfill the Old Testament sacrifices?

4. What is transubstantiation?

5. How is the Eucharist a sacrifice?

Quiz

True/False

1. ____ The fundamental element of any Old Testament sacrifice was the offering of thanksgiving.
2. ____ Circumcision was a sacrifice associated with the covenant with Moses.
3. ____ To prepare the Israelites to enter into a covenant with him, God saved them by means of a sacrificial paschal lamb.
4. ____ The sacrifices of the Mosaic Law couldn't effect what they represented.
5. ____ The Feeding of the Five Thousand was a sign that Jesus would feed all people.
6. ____ Like the New Covenant, the Old Testament animal sacrifices stipulated that both flesh and blood had to be consumed.
7. ____ The ancient Passover meal involved three cups of wine.
8. ____ What a thing is beneath its appearance is referred to as its "accidents."
9. ____ Transubstantiation takes places in the Mass when the priest says "this is my body" and "this is my blood."
10. ____ The Eucharistic sacrifice replaces Jesus's sacrifice on the cross.

Questions for Discussion

1. Have you ever made a sacrifice to God for yourself or for someone else? What kind of sacrifice did you make? Why did you make it?

2. Why do some people find it hard to believe that Jesus is truly present in the Eucharist? How can we explain transubstantiation in a way that makes sense to ordinary people?

Essay Topics / Further Study

1. Choose one of the Old Testament covenants to revisit. Is there an element of sacrifice involved in the covenant? If so, how does it prefigure one of the sacraments? Is there any element of that sacrament that refers back to the Old Testament covenant?

2. Research the different types of sacrifice that the Israelites offered. What did different sacrifices mean? Who could offer them?

3. Write a firsthand account of the Feeding of the Five Thousand. What did you see, hear, and experience? As a first-century Jew, what would this miraculous event mean to you?

4. Recent studies have shown that not all Catholics believe in the Real Presence of Jesus in the Eucharist. In the most persuasive way you can, explain transubstantiation and how the Eucharist relates back to Jesus's death on the cross. In closing, add what the Real Presence means to you personally.

5. Many saints have written about the importance of receiving Holy Communion. Find and study the writing of a saint on the Eucharist and summarize what you have learned.

Part IV: Chapter 2

Living the Sacrament

Memory Verse

> He who eats my flesh and drinks my blood has eternal life, and I will raise him up at the last day. For my flesh is food indeed, and my blood is drink indeed.
>
> —John 6:54–55

Key Terms

Gathering

Liturgy of the Word

Offertory

Anaphora

Preface

Epiclesis

Institution Narrative

Anamnesis

Intercessions

Communion

Dismissal

State of grace

Viaticum

Tabernacle

Monstrance

Adoration

Questions for Review

1. What are the six basic parts of the Mass?

2. Can the Eucharist ever be consecrated outside of the Mass?

3. Who can and cannot receive Communion? Why?

4. What commandments of Christ does the Eucharist fulfill?

5. What are the effects in our soul of receiving the Eucharist?

Quiz

1. There are six basic parts of the Mass, the first of which is _____.

2. In the part of the Mass called_____, the Sacred Scriptures are read and then explained in a homily.

3. The _____ is when the Church calls down the Holy Spirit on the bread and wine to be turned into the Body and Blood of Christ.

4. The _____ recalls what God has done in the sacrifice of the Mass.

5. The only minister who can celebrate the Eucharist is _____.

6. In the Latin Rite, the bread used for the Eucharist must be _____.

7. The _____ can never be interrupted once they have started, even for the gravest of necessities.

8. In order to receive Communion, one must be a baptized Catholic, be in a state of grace, and _____.

9. When the Eucharist is offered to a dying person, it is referred to as _____.

10. Catholics can worship the Eucharist outside of Mass through _____.

Questions for Discussion

1. What is the best thing you remember about your First Holy Communion? If you have not already received First Holy Communion, have you ever been to someone else's First Holy Communion? Why did people make such a big deal out of that day?

2. Have you ever spent time with Jesus in the Eucharist outside of Sunday Mass? If so, describe. What did you do? What was it like? How did it help you? Is there any way you could make this a regular habit? If not, how do you think that doing so might change you?

Essay Topics / Further Study

1. For each of the six basic parts of the Mass, find where Scripture is used in that part.

2. Using a Roman missal, read through the entirety of the Anaphora. Reflect on what these prayers present. How do they summarize and represent Catholic teaching?

3. Prepare a short explanation for non-Catholics on who can receive Communion and why. Why is it so important to be able to invite non-Catholics to Mass yet still make Catholic teaching on eligibility for receiving Communion so clear?

4. Do you or your parents know anyone who received *Viaticum* before dying? Why do you think it is so important for Catholics to receive Communion before dying, if possible?

5. Write a personal reflection on what the Eucharist has done in your own life. Have you been able to see the effects of the Eucharist in your life?

Part V

Penance and Reconciliation

Part V: Chapter 1

Understanding the Sacrament

Memory Verse

> Then Peter came up and said to him, "Lord, how often shall my brother sin against me, and I forgive him? As many as seven times?" Jesus said to him, "I do not say to you seven times, but seventy times seven."
>
> —Matthew 18:21–22

Key Terms

Atonement

Scapegoat

Forgiveness

Divination

Order of Penitents

Remission

Indulgence

Questions for Review

1. What role did the prophets of ancient Israel play in helping people understand their sins?

2. What role did the priests of ancient Israel play in helping people atone for their sins?

3. How did Jesus fulfill the roles of both prophet and priest in regard to sin?

4. What power regarding sin did Jesus give to his apostles?

5. What are indulgences and how do they help us?

Quiz

1. In the Old Testament, people in relationship with God followed a pattern of:
    A. confrontation, sin, confession, forgiveness.
    B. sin, confrontation, confession, forgiveness.
    C. sin, confession, forgiveness, confrontation.

2. After envying his brother's righteousness and committing murder, Cain:
    A. confesses his sin.
    B. is forgiven by God.
    C. went away from God's presence.

3. When we commit a serious sin, we die a spiritual death by:
    A. the loss of the Holy Sprit's presence.
    B. being denied all the sacraments.
    C. confessing without remorse.

4. God used prophets to help Israel:
   A. understand they had sinned.
   B. understand when God had forgiven them.
   C. both understand when they had sinned and when God had forgiven them.

5. The liturgy of _____ represented the repentance of the people of Israel.
   A. Passover
   B. Hanukkah
   C. Atonement

6. Jesus gave the power to forgive sins to:
   A. Mary.
   B. the disciples.
   C. the High Priest.

7. In the early Church, those who confessed sin were enrolled in _____ for a number of years.
   A. the Order of Excommunicates.
   B. the Order of Reprobates.
   C. the Order of Penitents.

8. A remission of the temporal punishment of sin is called:
   A. a libellus.
   B. an indulgence.
   C. a canon.

9. The practice of private confession developed under the influence of:
   A. Irish monks.
   B. the Church Fathers.
   C. St. Paul.

10. Indulgences are not a substitute for Reconciliation but:
    A. complement and complete the sacrament.
    B. amplify and strengthen the sacrament.
    C. replace and repair the sacrament.

Questions for Discussion

1. Have you ever "hidden" from God when you have committed a sin? If so, what about God's love and mercy were you having a hard time seeing?

2. Have you ever thought about gaining an indulgence? How could you make indulgences a more regular part of your life with God?

Essay Questions / Further Study

1. Research the origin of private confession. Contrast that with the practice of public confession. What are the advantages of each?

2. In this chapter, we looked at the pattern of sin first seen with Adam and Eve. Find and write about another Old Testament example that exemplifies the pattern of sin and forgiveness.

3. Is the liturgy of Atonement still celebrated by Jews today? Research how this holy day is observed.

4. Find two New Testament examples of Jesus forgiving sins. Is the pattern we saw in the Old Testament discernable in these examples? How does Jesus's forgiveness of sin differ from what we saw in the Old Testament?

5. Summarize the assigned reading from this chapter (CCC 1422–1498). How does the Catechism's teaching change your understanding of the sacrament of Reconciliation?

Part V: Chapter 2

Living the Sacrament

Memory Verse

> I will give you the keys of the kingdom of heaven, and whatever you bind on earth will be bound in heaven, and whatever you loose on earth will be loosed in heaven.
>
> —Matthew 16:19

Key Terms

Confession

Contrition

Satisfaction

Attrition

Seal of confession

Absolution

General confession

General absolution

Conversion

Questions for Review

1. Name and define each of the three "parts" of confession.

2. What is the difference between perfect and imperfect contrition?

3. Who is the minister of the sacrament of Penance and Reconciliation?

4. Why do we need to make satisfaction for our sins?

5. What is the difference between general confession and general absolution? Under what circumstances can general absolution be offered?

Quiz

1. The three "parts" of Penance are contrition, confession, and absolution.

2. Imperfect contrition is also called attrition.

3. Attrition obtains the remission of sins.

4. True contrition is motivated by love of God.

5. A priest can only violate the seal of confession if he needs to report a crime.

6. Remission is the process of repairing relationships damaged through our sin.

7. In danger of death, even a priest in bad standing with the Church can hear confessions.

8. We receive forgiveness in confession when the priest speaks the words of absolution.

9. When one receives general absolution, they must make a sacramental confession as soon as possible.

10. We can repair the damage done by sin through prayer, fasting, and almsgiving.

Questions for Discussion

1. Do you struggle with going to confession regularly? Why or why not?
2. Even though going to confession can feel hard or embarrassing at first, many people feel deep relief and joy afterward. Where does that joy come from? How can you share it with others in your life?

Essay Topics / Further Study

1. Imagine you have a friend who is anxious about going to confession. Write a letter of encouragement explaining all of the reasons why it is good to go to confession and why they should not be afraid.
2. Research how it is possible for someone who is deaf to receive the sacrament of Reconciliation.
3. In danger of death, any priest is given permission to hear confessions. Research whether excommunicated priests can hear confessions in this situation. What about laicized priests?
4. With the help of the selected reading from the Council of Trent, explain the difference between the sacraments of Penance and Baptism. What similarities do you think these two sacraments share?

Part VI

ANOINTING OF THE SICK

Part VI: Chapter 1

Understanding the Sacrament

Memory Verse

> Blessed be the God and Father of our Lord Jesus Christ, the Father of mercies and God of all comfort, who comforts us in all our affliction, so that we may be able to comfort those who are in any affliction, with the comfort with which we ourselves are comforted by God.
>
> —2 Corinthians 1:3–4

Key Terms

Barrenness

Leprosy

Ritual cleansing

Immaculate Conception

Presbyter

Oil

Supplication

Extreme Unction

Questions for Review

1. In the Old Testament, what did physical healing signify?

2. What two material substances were used in the Israelites' ritual cleansing ceremonies for lepers?

3. What does Jesus show us through the miraculous healings he performed?

4. Where in Sacred Scripture is the sacrament of the Anointing of the Sick mentioned? How are we told it was celebrated by the apostles?

5. What is the danger of waiting until the moment of death for the sacrament of the Anointing of the Sick?

Quiz

1. The Anointing of the Sick can also be referred to as the sacrament of _____.

2. We see from Adam and Eve that sin causes _____.

3. The ritual cleansings of the Old Testament did not cause healings or forgiveness of sin, they only _____ healing and forgiveness.

4. Through Mary's Immaculate Conception, _____ itself was healed.

5. Through his miraculous healings, Jesus shows that he is _____.

6. A _____ in Scripture is someone of priestly dignity.

7. Unlike in other Sacraments, the words used in the sacrament of Anointing of the sick are not a _____ from Jesus.

8. The sacrament of Anointing of the Sick is not a guarantee of physical healing but promises to _____ the sick.

9. The sacrament of the Anointing of the Sick prepares people to_____.

10. When someone is nearing death, the Church offers the sacraments of _____, _____, and _____.

Questions for Discussion

1. Have you ever been seriously injured or sick? If so, how was your illness or injury frustrating? How did God help you? If not, have you ever cared for someone else who was? What was that experience like?

2. Have you ever been in a situation when you needed to receive the sacrament of Anointing of the Sick? If so, what was it like? If not, how can you prepare yourself for now so that if such a situation ever arises, you're ready to accept all the graces that God wants to give you through it?

Essay Topics / Further Study

1. In the Old Testament, there was a perception that physical suffering was caused by sin or God's disapproval. What do you think it would be like to live with that understanding? What would Jesus's message mean to you if you had been raised with an understanding of illness being caused by sin?

2. Leprosy is a devastating disease that we hear about often in Scripture. Study the life of St. Damien of Molokai. In what ways did he model his life after Jesus?

3. Choose one New Testament episode of physical healing from the life of Jesus. Using BibliaClerus.org or another Catholic Scripture commentary, recount what the Church Fathers believed Jesus was trying to convey through this act of healing.

4. Compare the sacrament of Anointing of the Sick to the sacrament of Penance and Reconciliation. In what ways are the two sacraments similar? What makes them unique?

5. Summarize the assigned reading from this chapter (CCC 1499–1535). How does the teaching of the Catechism enhance your understanding of the sacrament of the Anointing of the Sick?

Part VI: Chapter 2

Living the Sacrament

Memory Verse

> Now I rejoice in my sufferings for your sake, and in my flesh I complete what is lacking in Christ's afflictions for the sake of his body, that is, the church.
> —Colossians 1:24

Key Terms

Second Vatican Council

Periculose

Viaticum

Resurrection of the body

Euthanasia

Questions for Review

1. How did the celebration of the Anointing of the Sick change after the Second Vatican Council?

2. What is Viaticum and when is it administered?

3. What are the effects of the Anointing of the Sick for those who are very ill?

4. What are the effects of the Anointing of the Sick for those who are dying?

5. How many times can you receive the Anointing of the Sick?

Quiz

1. The Second Vatican Council changed the _____ of the Anointing of the Sick.
   A. teaching
   B. practice
   C. requirements

2. The changes to the sacrament of the Anointing of the Sick made at the Second Vatican Council were for the sake of:
   A. increasing active participation.
   B. updating an outdated ritual.
   C. correcting an error in teaching.

3. The Church's term for those who are seriously ill is:
   A. periculose.
   B. viaticum.
   C. gravitas.

4. A person can receive the sacrament of Anointing of the Sick:
   A. once.
   B. twice.
   C. multiple times.

5. The celebration of _____ can be added to the sacrament of Anointing of the Sick.
   A. the Liturgy of the Word
   B. Baptism
   C. the Mass

6. The Church prepares the dying by giving them the sacrament of _____ last.
   A. Anointing of the Sick
   B. Reconciliation
   C. the Eucharist

7. The Anointing of the sick:
   A. guarantees physical healing.
   B. forgives sin.
   C. offers a kind of baptism.

8. Anointing fills us with the Holy Sprit:
   A. and strengthens us to face sickness and death.
   B. but does not forgive our sins.
   C. and is administered after Viaticum.

9. The goal of the sacrament of Anointing of the sick is:
   A. to heal our physical illness.
   B. to renew our Baptism.
   C. to prepare us to go home to heaven.

10. Ending life prematurely through medical means is referred to as:
    A. euthanasia.
    B. fratricide.
    C. infirmity.

Questions for Discussion

1. What are some of the temptations those who are gravely ill or injured can face?

2. How could the graces of the Anointing of the Sick help us face those temptations?

Essay Topics / Further Study

1. Do you know someone who has received the sacrament of Anointing of the Sick? What do you believe the effects of the sacrament were?

2. The selected reading from Pope Benedict offers a beautiful teaching on how Jesus ministers to the sick. What hope would you offer someone who is suffering from terminal or chronic illness?

3. Research all of the sacramentals that are used in the sacrament of Anointing of the Sick. What significance do the prayers and actions of the sacrament have?

4. Construct a dialog between yourself and an elderly person approaching death who has fallen away from the Church. Explain to them what the sacrament of the Anointing of the Sick is and what benefits it has for them.

5. In our world today, many people believe that suffering is to be avoided at all costs. How does this differ from a Catholic understanding of suffering? Explain what euthanasia is and why the Church is against this practice.

Part VII

HOLY ORDERS

Part VII: Chapter 1

Understanding the Sacrament

Memory Verse

> But you are a chosen race, a royal priesthood, a holy nation, God's own people, that you may declare the wonderful deeds of him who called you out of darkness into his marvelous light.
>
> —1 Peter 2:9

Key Terms

Holy Orders

Ordination

Priest

Aaron

High Priest

Holy Anointing Oil

Levites

Apostle

Bishops

Presbyters

Deacons

Peter

Keys of the kingdom

Papal primacy

Papacy

Questions for Review

1. What is the most basic function of any priest, Catholic or not?

2. What priesthood did God establish in the Old Testament? Who could be priests?

3. What are the three different ways that men can be sacramentally ordained to participate in Jesus's priesthood? Name and define each.

4. What special task did Jesus entrust to Peter?

5. Who carries on that task today?

Quiz

True/False

1. ____ A priest is defined as "one who offers sacrifice."
2. ____ When Aaron abused the sacrificial office, God removed him from priestly service.
3. ____ "Levite" means "one who has been sent."
4. ____ Presbyters receive a complete sharing in the apostolic ministry.
5. ____ Deacons assist the bishops in governing the Church.
6. ____ Bishops exercise Jesus's offices of prophet, priest, and king.
7. ____ By the year AD 100, we have evidence that the Church was ordaining bishops.
8. ____ The keys of the kingdom are a symbol of perfection.
9. ____ Papal primacy is the understanding that only those bishops, priests, and deacons in union with the pope speak for and are sent directly by Christ.
10. ____ The papacy is a sacrament.

Questions for Discussion

1. Have you ever known a priest who brought Jesus especially close to you? How could you see Jesus working through him?

2. How much do you know about our present pope? How does he inspire you or challenge you?

Essay Topics / Further Study

1. What is another type of priesthood outside of the Catholic Church? How does it differ from the Catholic priesthood?

2. Using Scripture and Old Testament commentaries found online, make a list of the rules that priests from the tribe of Levi had to follow. Are any of these rules similar to what Catholic priests must follow today?

3. Read the whole story of Phinehas and Hophni in the book of Samuel. Does this story bear any similarity to the actions of priests causing scandal in the Church? How does God deal with Phinehas and Hophni, and what can the Church today learn from this story?

4. Using as many examples from the New Testament that you can find, list similarities between St. Peter and a pope who has held the office of the papacy in your lifetime.

5. Choose one of the three degrees of Holy Orders—the episcopate, presbyterate, or diaconate—to study further. What is entailed in their ordination process? Have you witnessed the exercise of that office in your parish or diocese? How do you see it as an extension of the work of the apostles?

Part VII: Chapter 2

Living the Sacrament

Memory Verse

> So then, brothers and sisters, stand firm and hold fast to the traditions that you were taught by us, either by word of mouth or by our letter.
>
> —2 Thessalonians 2:15

Key Terms

Holy Orders

Collegiality

Celibacy

Miter

Crosier

Insignia

In persona Christi capitis

Tithe

Questions for Review

1. What gesture is central to the ordination of a priest?

2. Who is the minister of the sacrament of Holy Orders and has the authority to ordain a priest?

3. How is Holy Orders like Baptism and Confirmation?

4. Does the personal holiness of a priest or bishop affect his ability to baptize, celebrate the Eucharist, forgive sins, or confect any other sacrament?

5. What guarantees the priest's ability to carry out his sacramental ministry?

Quiz

1. The minister of the sacrament of Holy Orders is always a _____.

2. Following the example of Christ, only _____ can be candidates for Holy Orders.

3. Men who are going to be ordained must first be _____.

4. Since time immemorial the clergy have practiced the custom of _____.

5. In the Latin Rite, ordination includes a process of a candidate being presented, chosen, _____, and prepared through prayer.

6. The ring, miter, and the crosier are called the bishop's _____.

7. The principle effect of the sacrament of Holy Orders is the conferral of an _____ _____.

8. The first degree of Holy Orders is _____.

9. The character conferred on a priest enables him to act _____ *capitis*.

10. The Church explicitly acknowledges that the faithful have an obligation to contribute to the material needs of the ordained by _____.

Questions for Discussion

1. What are some ways in which you and your family could work together to support those who serve you in sacramental ministry with your prayer, service, and generosity?

2. If you are a young man, have you ever prayed about a vocation to the priesthood? Why or why not? What are some ways we can support and encourage those who might be called to this vocation?

Essay Topics / Further Study

1. Interview a man who has received the sacrament of Holy Orders. What does the sacrament mean to him?

2. Research and explain what a bishop's ring, miter, and crosier symbolize.

3. The Church has often been criticized for the practice of priestly celibacy. Study further reasons for this practice. Why is the practice of celibacy so important?

4. Write a letter to your priest or bishop thanking him for his exercise of Holy Orders. Explain how you see him fulfilling the responsibilities of the office.

5. Write a brief biography of a saint who had been ordained to the diaconate, priesthood, or episcopacy.

Part VIII

Holy Matrimony

Part VIII: Chapter 1

Understanding the Sacrament

Memory Verse

> And I will take you for my wife forever; I will take you for my wife in righteousness and in justice, in steadfast love, and in mercy. I will take you for my wife in faithfulness; and you shall know the Lord.
>
> —Hosea 2:19–20

Key Terms

Marriage

Divorce

Prohibitory impediment

Diriment impediment

Consanguinity

Affinity

Cohabitation

Annulment

Convalidation

Pauline privilege

Petrine privilege

Questions for Review

1. How is marriage different from other sacraments?

2. What was God's original plan for marriage?

3. How did marriage change after Jesus established the Church?

4. What does Jesus teach about divorce?

5. What are the four impediments to marriage established by God? What are the six impediments established by the Church?

Quiz

1. Jesus did not _____ marriage.
    A. make a sacrament of
    B. institute
    C. think highly of

PART VIII: CHAPTER 1
UNDERSTANDING THE SACRAMENT

2. The Mosaic Law _____ divorce, but did not _____ it.
   A. permitted, promote
   B. commanded, require
   C. mentioned, regulate

3. Jesus teaches what Deuteronomy teaches about divorce, except:
   A. he does not allow for divorce under any circumstances.
   B. through the lens of canon law.
   C. from the perspective of the man.

4. _____ impediments are established directly by God.
   A. Prohibitory
   B. Diriment
   C. Affinity

5. According to Canon Law, the minimum age of marriage for women is:
   A. fourteen.
   B. eighteen.
   C. twenty-one.

6. The person designated to initiate proceedings for a Declaration of Nullity is called a:
   A. canon lawyer.
   B. sponsor.
   C. promoter of justice.

7. After diriment impediments are removed, a civilly married couple can have their marriage blessed by the Church in an act called:
   A. convalidation.
   B. validation.
   C. regularization.

8. A decree of annulment declares:
   A. that an existing marriage is dissolved.
   B. that a marriage was never valid.
   C. that one or both parties is ineligible to marry.

9. When a marriage is not between two baptized people, it can be:
   A. dissolved in favor of the faith.
   B. dissolved by a divorce.
   C. replaced by cohabitation.

10. The appropriate time to seek a civil divorce is:
    A. after an annulment has been granted.
    B. before an annulment has been granted.
    C. after both parties are in new relationships.

Questions for Discussion

1. Give an example of a healthy marriage you have witnessed. How could you see Jesus active in that relationship?

2. What do the various impediments to marriage teach us about the grace that God wants to give us in marriage? What makes marriage different from other relationships?

Essay Topics / Further Study

1. Choose one Old Testament married couple to study. What can you learn about marriage from their example?

2. Write a first-person account of the wedding feast at Cana. What would you see, hear, and experience? How would the bride and groom react to Jesus's miracle? What about the other guests?

3. Both the Old and New Testaments are clear about divorce and remarriage. Using Scripture and the Catechism, explain the Church's teaching on divorce.

4. Choose one diriment impediment to research further. Using the Code of Canon Law, found online, explain why this impediment prevents someone from entering into marriage.

5. Choose one prohibitory impediment to research further. Using the Code of Canon Law, found online, explain why this impediment prevents someone from entering into marriage.

Part VIII: Chapter 2

Living the Sacrament

Memory Verse

> Husbands, love your wives, just as Christ loved the church and gave himself up for her, in order to make her holy by cleansing her with the washing of water by the word, so as to present the church to himself in splendor, without a spot or wrinkle or anything of the kind—yes, so that she may be holy and without blemish.
>
> —Ephesians 5:25–27

Key Terms

Consent

Bond

Domestic church

Marriage supper of the lamb

Consecrated life

Vocation

Theology of the body

Questions for Review

1. What are the essential elements that must be present in a wedding ceremony for a marriage to take place?

2. Who are the ministers of the sacrament?

3. What is the primary effect of the sacrament of Matrimony?

4. What is the domestic church?

5. Does a change in one's emotions or feelings about one's spouse change the nature of the bond between them?

Quiz

True/False

1. ____ Consent is a necessary requirement of what makes a marriage.
2. ____ A priest or deacon is the minister of the sacrament of Matrimony.
3. ____ Marriage has a naturally private character.
4. ____ The primary effect of the sacrament of Matrimony is that it creates freedom between the husband and wife.
5. ____ Marriage both points to and makes present between the spouses the love that Christ has for the Church.
6. ____ The domestic church is the context in which most people live out their relationship with God.
7. ____ Parents are not responsible for their child's vocation.

8. ____ Consecrated life is a sacrament.
9. ____ Individuals can appropriate the graces of marriage by first preparing for it through prayer, discernment, and virtue.
10. ____ Couples are called to be open to life but not necessarily to raise their children in the Church.

Questions for Discussion

1. What challenges can make fidelity to one's marriage vows difficult? How can couples overcome those challenges?

2. What virtues do husbands and wives need to possess in order to be good spouses and remain faithful to one another? How can you start acquiring those virtues now?

Essay Topics / Further Study

1. Interview your parents or another married couple. What do they remember about their exchange of vows specifically? Did they know at the time that "consent makes a marriage"?

2. Search online for Church documents that teach about the domestic church. After reading, summarize what the Church teaches. How does this change your understanding of your own family?

3. The selected reading from Pope St. John Paul II explains the meaning of marriage. In your own words, summarize the points made by the Holy Father.

4. Using Scripture, the Catechism, and the lives of the saints, make a list of all the advice the Church gives married couples. List as many points as possible.

5. Research a canonized saint who was married. How did they live out their vocation? What can other married people learn about marriage from their example?

Final Exam

_____ / 100

Matching

2 points each

A. Instrumental cause
B. Sanctifying grace
C. Sacrament
D. Indulgence
E. Character
F. Contrition
G. Original Sin
H. Periculose
I. Actual grace
J. Attrition
K. Extreme Unction
L. Transubstantiation
M. Apostle
N. Concupiscence
O. Protoevangelium
P. Deicide
Q. Satisfaction
R. Viaticum
S. Adoration
T. Primary cause
U. Gathering
V. Prophets
W. Messiah
X. Catechumens
Y. Exorcism

_____ 1. Means "anointed one"
_____ 2. The act of killing God is called
_____ 3. Anointed to speak the words of God to the Israelites
_____ 4. The spiritual mark Baptism leaves on us and can never be taken away
_____ 5. Means "one who is sent"
_____ 6. An inclination toward sin
_____ 7. A remission of the temporal punishment of sin is called
_____ 8. Another name for Anointing of the Sick
_____ 9. Imperfect contrition
_____ 10. A habitual gift, a stable and supernatural disposition that perfects the soul itself to enable it to live with God, to act by his love
_____ 11. Efficacious signs of grace, instituted by Christ and entrusted to the Church, by which divine life is dispensed to us.
_____ 12. The first part of the Mass
_____ 13. The Church's term for those who are seriously ill
_____ 14. The object or person who acts in the administering of the sacraments
_____ 15. Inherited from Adam and Eve
_____ 16. When one substance, that of bread or wine, passes to the next, that of the Body and Blood of Jesus
_____ 17. The process of repairing relationships damaged through our sin
_____ 18. Obtains the remission of sins
_____ 19. Included in the rite of Baptism
_____ 20. The grace that God gives us that enables us to act
_____ 21. The final Eucharist offered to a dying person
_____ 22. The worship of the Eucharist outside of Mass
_____ 23. The promise of a savior that is issued immediately after the first sin is called
_____ 24. Those preparing to be received into the Church
_____ 25. The tool through which a sacrament is administered

Short Answer

5 points each

1. How did God prepare humanity for a sacramental relationship with himself in the Old Testament?

2. Into what three categories does the Church typically divide the sacraments?

3. What is a baptism of desire? What is a baptism of blood?

4. Name three effects of Confirmation.

5. List the seven gifts of the Holy Spirit and the twelve fruits of the Holy Spirit.

6. What are the six basic parts of the Mass?

7. Who can and cannot receive Communion? Why?

8. Name and define each of the three "parts" of confession.

9. What is the difference between perfect and imperfect contrition?

10. What are the three different ways that men can be sacramentally ordained to participate in Jesus's priesthood? Name and define each.

Answer Key

Part I: Chapter 1—Definition of Sacrament

Questions for Review

1. What was the meaning of the word *sacramentum* in the ancient Roman world?

In ancient Rome, *sacramentum* was a legal term referring to a bond posted at the beginning of a lawsuit as the proof that payment could be made if the lawsuit was lost. It also referred to the oath taken at the beginning of military service.

2. What is the difference between the sacraments of the Church and the customs of Roman soldiers?

The difference between the sacraments of the Church and the customs of Roman soldiers is the Holy Spirit, who is the transformative power behind the words of the sacraments. Also, customs of the Roman soldiers do not affect what they signify, while sacraments make the thing they point to happen.

3. What is sanctifying grace?

The Catechism says that sanctifying grace is "an habitual gift, a stable and supernatural disposition that perfects the soul itself to enable it to live with God, to act by his love."

4. How does the Church define "sacrament"?

The Church defines sacraments as "efficacious signs of grace, instituted by Christ and entrusted to the Church, by which divine life is dispensed to us."

5. Why do we call the Church "the universal sacrament of salvation"?

We call the Church the universal sacrament of salvation because it not only points to salvation, but also makes salvation happen.

Quiz

True/False
1. True
2. False: The Holy Spirit
3. False: actual grace
4. True
5. False: It is also a habitual gift

6. True
7. True
8. False: not "properly speaking" is the Church a sacrament
9. False: Tertullian
10. True

Part I: Chapter 2—Redemption Is Mediated Through the Sacraments

Questions for Review

1. What is the difference between a primary cause and an instrumental cause (in regards to the administering of a sacrament)?

The primary cause is the object or person who acts; the instrumental cause is the tool through which the action is done.

2. How did God prepare humanity for a sacramental relationship with himself in the Old Testament?

God prepared humanity for a sacramental relationship with himself in the Old Testament through a series of covenants. Each covenant included some sign or symbol that pointed out what God was doing in that covenant and prepared us to receive the sacraments that Jesus was going to establish.

3. What is the difference between the covenantal signs in the Old Testament and the sacraments of the New Testament?

The covenantal signs in the Old Testament were not sacraments properly speaking, and so their actions did not make things happen in the same way that sacraments do.

4. What happened to the Old Testament signs when Jesus came?

When Jesus came, the Old Testament signs passed away.

5. Into what three categories does the Church typically divide the sacraments?

The Church typically divides the sacraments into the categories of initiation, healing, and service of Communion.

Quiz

1. God's words
2. primary cause
3. instrumental cause
4. covenants
5. sacraments

ANSWER KEY

6. prefigured
7. passed away
8. the apostles
9. of healing
10. Communion

Part II: Chapter 1 — Understanding the Sacrament

Questions for Review

1. Before the Fall, what could Adam and Eve learn from water about their relationship with God?

Before the Fall, Adam and Eve could learn that water was a sign of their relationship with God: just as they needed water to live (to drink and to water their crops), so, too, did they depend on God for their whole sustenance, who protected them from floods and provided enough water from above.

2. After the Fall, how did God use water to bring about purification from sin? Give two examples.

After the Fall, God purified the human race of sin through the Great Flood, which brought about the destruction of all but the righteous Noah and his family, and through the parting of the Red Sea, which put to death the Egyptians and their sins by which they held the Israelites captive.

3. Why was Jesus baptized?

Jesus was baptized to take our repentance upon himself and to be the first among us to repent.

4. Is Baptism necessary for salvation?

Baptism is necessary for salvation, as is evidenced by Jesus's command, the example of the early Church, and Catholic teaching.

5. What is a baptism of desire? What is a baptism of blood?

Baptism of desire is an occasion on which God might choose to offer someone the same grace that they would have received if they had been baptized, if that person had an unwavering desire for Baptism and if they did not delay in requesting Baptism from the Church, but was unable to receive the actual sacrament because of their untimely death. Baptism of blood is an occasion on which God might choose to offer someone baptismal grace without the sacrament of Baptism, if that person had unwavering faith and if they offered themselves and were killed out of others' hatred for faith in Christ.

Quiz

1. B
2. A

3. A
4. C
5. C
6. B
7. A
8. C
9. B
10. C

Part II: Chapter 2—Living the Sacrament

Questions for Review

1. What are the necessary words that must be spoken in Baptism?

The necessary words that must be spoken in Baptism are "N., I baptize you in the name of the Father, and of the Son, and of the Holy Spirit."

2. Who ordinarily administers the sacrament? Are there any exceptions to this?

The sacrament is administered ordinarily by a bishop, priest, or deacon. If someone is in danger of death, any person can serve as a minister of Baptism, even if that person has not yet been baptized.

3. What types of sins are forgiven in Baptism?

In Baptism, both original sin and personal sins are forgiven.

4. What "new beginnings" does Baptism mark?

Baptism marks a new beginning through the forgiveness of sins, life as a new creation in the Holy Spirit, the presence of sanctifying grace, and membership in the Body of Christ.

5. What do we call the spiritual mark Baptism leaves on us? Can that mark ever be taken away?

The spiritual mark Baptism leaves on us is called a *character*. That mark can never be taken away from us.

Quiz

True/False
1. True
2. True
3. False: two gifts, a white garment and a candle
4. False: parents have a responsibility to choose Baptism for their children
5. False: it is a state that we inherit from Adam and Eve
6. True

7. True
8. False: sanctifying grace
9. True
10. False: character

Part III: Chapter 1 — Understanding the Sacrament

Questions for Review

1. In the ancient world, what did oil symbolize?

In the ancient world, oil symbolized nourishment, health, and beauty.

2. In the Old Testament, what were the three categories of people anointed by oil, and why were they anointed?

In the Old Testament, priests, kings, and prophets were anointed with oil. Priests were anointed so they could offer ritual sacrifice and assist the Israelites in living out their relationship with God. Kings were anointed to govern Israel. Prophets were anointed to speak the words of God to the people of Israel, about the present and the future.

3. Who was anointed in the Gospels?

In the Gospels, the disciples were anointed.

4. What is received in Confirmation?

In Confirmation, the recipient receives an increase in the gifts of the Holy Spirit.

5. For what do the gifts we receive in Confirmation prepare us?

The gifts we receive in Confirmation prepare us for bearing public witness to the faith and engaging in spiritual combat.

Quiz

1. water
2. the Holy Spirit
3. nourishment
4. Kings
5. Prophets
6. Priests
7. anointed person/one
8. *Christos* or Christ
9. West
10. East

Part III: Chapter 2—Living the Sacrament

Questions for Review

1. What are the essential words that must be spoken in the sacrament of Confirmation?

The essential words that must be spoken in the sacrament of Confirmation are, "Be sealed with the Holy Spirit."

2. Who is the original minister of Confirmation? Who else can administer the sacrament?

The original minister of Confirmation is the bishop, the successor of the apostles. Priests can also administer the sacrament (but the chrism that is used must be blessed by the bishop).

3. Is Confirmation necessary for salvation? Why or why not?

Confirmation is not necessary for salvation. It is necessary for perfecting our salvation, but we can still get to heaven without Confirmation.

4. Name three effects of Confirmation.

Three effects of Confirmation are completing the grace of our Baptism, raising us to spiritual maturity, and empowering us with mature spiritual responsibility. (Other possible answer: imprinting a new sacramental character on our souls.)

5. What can affect the extent to which we benefit from the graces of Confirmation?

Our level of interior cooperation can affect the extent to which we benefit from the graces of Confirmation.

Quiz

1. C
2. B
3. A
4. C
5. A
6. C
7. B
8. A
9. B
10. A

Part VI: Chapter 1 — Understanding the Sacrament

Questions for Review

1. What is the fundamental element of a sacrifice?

The fundamental element of a sacrifice is the offering of life.

2. What could the sacrifices of the Old Testament not accomplish? What could they accomplish?

The sacrifices of the Old Testament could not offer the people's spiritual life to God. They could only represent the remembrance of God having given people spiritual life.

3. In what three ways did Jesus promise to fulfill the Old Testament sacrifices?

Jesus promised to fulfill the Old Testament sacrifices by providing a miraculous food that would feed all of his people, would do so continually, and would do so in such a way as would give them spiritual life.

4. What is transubstantiation?

Transubstantiation is when one substance, that of bread or wine, passes to the next, that of the Body and Blood of Jesus.

5. How is the Eucharist a sacrifice?

The Eucharist is a covenantal sacrifice in which the offering of Jesus's blood is renewed in an unbloody manner.

Quiz

True/False
1. False: The offering of life
2. False: Abraham
3. True
4. True
5. True
6. False: blood was forbidden from being consumed
7. False: four cups
8. False: substance
9. True
10. False: renews

Part IV: Chapter 2—Living the Sacrament

Questions for Review

1. What are the six basic parts of the Mass?

The six basic parts of the Mass are the Gathering, the Liturgy of the Word, the Offertory, the Anaphora (or Offering), Communion, and the Dismissal.

2. Can the Eucharist ever be consecrated outside of the Mass?

The Eucharist can never be consecrated outside of the Mass.

3. Who can and cannot receive Communion? Why?

Only those who are baptized, in a state of grace, and have prepared by fasting for one hour can receive Communion because these conditions reflect our unity with Jesus. Those who are not baptized or are not in a state of grace commit sacrilege if they take Communion.

4. What commandments of Christ does the Eucharist fulfill?

The Eucharist fulfills the greatest commandments of Jesus: to love God and to love our neighbor.

5. What are the effects in our soul of receiving the Eucharist?

The effects in our soul of receiving the Eucharist are the increase of charity in our hearts, forgiveness of venial sin and perseverance against mortal sin, union with the poor, and unity with God and neighbor.

Quiz

1. the Gathering
2. the Liturgy of the Word
3. Epiclesis
4. Anamnesis
5. a validly ordained priest
6. Options: made from wheat, unleavened
7. Words of Institution
8. have fasted for one hour
9. *viaticum*
10. Adoration

Part V: Chapter 1—Understanding the Sacrament

Questions for Review

1. What role did the prophets of ancient Israel play in helping people understand their sins?

The prophets of ancient Israel helped people understand their sins by inviting them to confess and pronouncing when God had forgiven them.

2. What role did the priests of ancient Israel play in helping people atone for their sins?

The priests of ancient Israel helped people atone for their sins by performing signs that represented the forgiveness that the people would receive if they sincerely repented from their sins.

3. How did Jesus fulfill the roles of both prophet and priest in regard to sin?

Jesus fulfilled the roles of both prophet and priest in regard to sin by pronouncing when God had already given forgiveness from sins, but he made this forgiveness happen, and he performed a sacrifice that represented the repentance of God's people, but performed one that actually caused it.

4. What power regarding sin did Jesus give to his apostles?

Jesus gave his apostles the authority to forgive sins.

5. What are indulgences and how do they help us?

Indulgences are "remissions before God of the temporal punishment due to sins whose guilt has already been forgiven." Indulgences forgive part or all of the temporal consequences of our sins. Indulgences help us by both complementing and completing the sacrament of Reconciliation.

Quiz

1. B
2. C
3. A
4. C
5. C
6. B
7. C
8. B
9. A
10. A

Part V: Chapter 2—Living the Sacrament

Questions for Review

1. Name and define each of the three "parts" of confession.

The three parts of Penance are contrition, confession, and satisfaction. Contrition is the "sorrow of the soul and detestation for the sin committed, together with the resolution not to sin again." Confession is the vocal disclosure of our sins to a priest in the sacrament of Penance and Reconciliation. Satisfaction is "making up for our sins," repairing our relationship with God, which we do through the penance we are assigned by the priest.

2. What is the difference between perfect and imperfect contrition?

Perfect contrition is complete contrition. It is sorrow for sins that comes from the right motivation, the love of God, and the desire to confess our sins as soon as possible. Imperfect sin, or "attrition," is not completed by the love of God, but rather the fear of God's punishment for sin instead.

3. Who is the minister of the sacrament of confession?

The minister of the sacrament of confession is any priest who has received the proper permission from his bishop to forgive sins.

4. Why do we need to make satisfaction for our sins?

We need to make satisfaction for our sins to repair our relationship with God, the Church, ourselves, and our neighbors.

5. What is the difference between general confession and general absolution? Under what circumstances can general absolution be offered?

General confession is a term used for the practice of confessing one's sins from a long period of time, rather than just the time between one's last confession. General absolution is absolution granted to a group of people all at once in a time of grave necessity. (General confession can also be understood in terms of general absolution: when a group, because of grave necessity, is invited by a priest to make some sign of contrition in order to receive general absolution.)

Quiz

1. False: contrition, confession, and satisfaction
2. True
3. False: Contrition
4. True
5. False: a priest can never break the seal of confession
6. False: Satisfaction

ANSWER KEY

7. True
8. True
9. True
10. True

Part VI: Chapter 1—Understanding the Sacrament

Questions for Review

1. In the Old Testament, what did physical healing signify?

In the Old Testament, physical healing signified a restoration of spiritual life and God's blessing.

2. What two material substances were used in the Israelites' ritual cleansing ceremonies for lepers?

Blood and oil were used in the Israelites' ritual cleansing ceremonies for lepers.

3. What does Jesus show us through the miraculous healings he performed?

Through the miraculous healings he performed, Jesus shows us that he is God.

4. Where in Sacred Scripture is the sacrament of the Anointing of the Sick mentioned? How are we told it was celebrated by the apostles?

In Mark 6:13 and James 5:14–15 the sacrament of the Anointing of the Sick is mentioned. We are told that the apostles celebrated the sacrament by calling for a priest, praying over the sick person, speaking the words of the prayer of Jesus, and anointing the sick person with oil.

5. What is the danger of waiting until the moment of death for the sacrament of the Anointing of the Sick?

The danger of waiting until the moment of death for the sacrament of the Anointing of the Sick is that many people on their deathbeds are not able to participate consciously in the reception of this sacrament. Waiting until the moment of death to administer the sacrament also leaves less of an opportunity for the healing effect of the sacrament to take place without a dramatic miracle happening.

Quiz

1. Extreme Unction
2. spiritual death
3. pointed to
4. human nature
5. God
6. Presbyter

7. direct statement
8. raise up/forgive the sins of
9. go home to heaven
10. Penance, Eucharist/Viaticum, Anointing of the Sick

Part VI: Chapter 2—Living the Sacrament

Questions for Review

1. How did the celebration of the Anointing of the Sick change after the Second Vatican Council?

After the Second Vatican Council, the celebration of the Anointing of the Sick changed by allowing people who were seriously sick, not just at the moment of death, to receive the sacrament.

2. What is Viaticum and when is it administered?

Viaticum is the last Eucharist given to someone before dying. It is administered after reception of the sacrament of Anointing of the Sick.

3. What are the effects of the Anointing of the Sick for those who are very ill?

For those who are very ill, the Anointing of the Sick unites us with the Blood of Christ, which fills us with the Holy Spirit. We are healed from the remnants of sin and forgiven of any remaining sins. We are strengthened to face the spiritual trials that sickness and death entail. The sacrament also prepares us to go home to heaven.

4. What are the effects of the Anointing of the Sick for those who are dying?

For those who are dying, the Anointing of the Sick has all of the effects as in those who are seriously ill, but it also prepares us to meet Jesus in heaven by uniting us to him in the reception of the Eucharist as Viaticum.

5. How many times can you receive the Anointing of the Sick?

One can receive the Anointing of the Sick repeatedly, when one becomes sick, when one becomes sick after recovering, or when a condition becomes graver.

Quiz

1. B
2. A
3. A
4. C
5. A
6. C

7. B
8. A
9. C
10. A

Part VII: Chapter 1—Understanding the Sacrament

Questions for Review

1. What is the most basic function of any priest, Catholic or not?

The most basic function of any priest, Catholic or not, is to offer sacrifice.

2. What priesthood did God establish in the Old Testament? Who could be priests?

God established a national priesthood as part of the Mosaic Law in the Old Testament. Moses's brother Aaron and Aaron's descendants could be priests.

3. What are the three different ways that men can be sacramentally ordained to participate in Jesus's priesthood? Name and define each.

Men can be sacramentally ordained to participate in Jesus's priesthood as bishops, presbyters, and deacons. Bishops, or the office of bishop, is the fulfillment of the apostolic office. Presbyters, or priests, sit in council with the bishops and assist them in teaching, sanctifying, and governing the Church. Deacons help priests in the fulfilment of their apostolic duties, particularly that of charitable service.

4. What special task did Jesus entrust to Peter?

Jesus entrusted Peter with the authority to speak on his behalf.

5. Who carries on that task today?

Today, the task to authoritatively speak on behalf of Christ is carried out by all bishops, priests, and deacons, in union with the pope.

Quiz

True/False
1. True
2. False: Phinehas and Hophni
3. False: Apostle
4. False: Bishops
5. False: Priests
6. True
7. True
8. False: authority

9. True
10. False: not a sacrament

Part VII: Chapter 2—Living the Sacrament

Questions for Review

1. What gesture is central to the ordination of a priest?

The gesture that is central to the ordination of a priest is the laying on of hands.

2. Who is the minister of the sacrament of Holy Orders and has the authority to ordain a priest?

Only a bishop has the authority to ordain a priest and the minister of the sacrament of Holy Orders is always a bishop.

3. How is Holy Orders like Baptism and Confirmation?

Like Baptism and Confirmation, Holy Orders imparts an indelible character on the recipient.

4. Does the personal holiness of a priest or bishop affect his ability to baptize, celebrate the Eucharist, forgive sins, or confect any other sacrament?

The personal holiness of a priest or bishop does not prevent him from confecting the sacraments.

5. What guarantees the priest's ability to carry out his sacramental ministry?

The sacramental character of the priesthood, rooted in the priesthood of Christ himself, guarantees a priest's ability to carry out his sacramental ministry.

Quiz

1. bishop
2. men
3. baptized
4. celibacy
5. instructed
6. insignia
7. indelible character
8. the diaconate
9. *in persona Christi*
10. tithing

Part VIII: Chapter 1—Understanding the Sacrament

Questions for Review

1. How is marriage different from other sacraments?

Marriage is different from other sacraments because Jesus did not institute it; rather, he raised it to the dignity of a sacrament.

2. What was God's original plan for marriage?

God's original plan for marriage was for Adam and Eve to bring forth children in a relationship with God and begin the evangelization of the whole earth by the spread of their domestic church.

3. How did marriage change after Jesus established the Church?

After Jesus established the Church, marriage pointed to Jesus's love for the Church and made that love happen here on earth in the Christian family.

4. What does Jesus teach about divorce?

Jesus teaches that whoever divorces his wife, unless because of adultery, makes his spouse into an adulteress, and that anyone who marries a divorced woman commits adultery.

5. What are the four impediments to marriage established by God? What are the six impediments established by the Church?

The four impediments to marriage established by God are being unable to consummate the marriage, being directly related by blood, being already married, and being unable to consent to marriage (due to either lack of knowledge or consent). The six impediments established by the Church are marrying an unbaptized person if you are baptized, having received the sacrament Holy Orders, having taken a "public perpetual vow of chastity in a religious institute," murdering one's own spouse or murdering another person's spouse in order to marry that person, marrying someone in the direct line of ascent or descent of someone with whom you have previously cohabitated outside of marriage, and marrying outside the Church.

Quiz

1. B
2. A
3. C
4. B
5. A
6. C
7. A

8. B
9. A
10. A

Part VIII: Chapter 2—Living the Sacrament

Questions for Review

1. What are the essential elements that must be present in a wedding ceremony for a marriage to take place?

The essential elements that must be present in a wedding ceremony for a marriage to take place are a baptized man and woman, a representative of the Church, two witnesses, and the exchange of matrimonial consent.

2. Who are the ministers of the sacrament?

The ministers of the sacrament of Matrimony are the man and woman.

3. What is the primary effect of the sacrament of Matrimony?

The primary effect of the sacrament of Matrimony is the indissoluble bond it creates between the husband and wife.

4. What is the domestic church?

The domestic church is a household's participation in the Church's sacramental life, which makes present the fulfillment of the greatest commandments and is the context in which the vast majority of people live out their relationship with God.

5. Does a change in one's emotions or feelings about one's spouse change the nature of the bond between them?

A change in one's emotions or feelings about one's spouse does not change the nature of the bond between husband and wife.

Quiz

1. True
2. False: The man and woman are the ministers
3. False: communal
4. False: it creates an indissoluble bond
5. True
6. True
7. False: Parents have a duty to encourage their child's vocation.
8. False: is not
9. True
10. False: Couples are called to both be open to life and to raise their children in the Church

Final Exam

Matching

2 points each

1. W
2. P
3. V
4. E
5. M
6. N
7. D
8. K
9. J
10. B
11. C
12. U
13. H
14. T
15. G
16. L
17. Q
18. F
19. Y
20. I
21. R
22. S
23. O
24. X
25. A

Short Answer

5 points each

1. How did God prepare humanity for a sacramental relationship with himself in the Old Testament?

God prepared humanity for a sacramental relationship with himself in the Old Testament through a series of covenants. Each covenant included some sign or symbol that pointed out what God was doing in that covenant and prepared us to receive the sacraments that Jesus was going to establish.

2. Into what three categories does the Church typically divide the sacraments?

The Church typically divides the sacraments into the categories of initiation, healing, and service of Communion.

3. What is a baptism of desire? What is a baptism of blood?

Baptism of desire is an occasion on which God might choose to offer someone the same grace that they would have received if they had been baptized, if that person had an unwavering desire for Baptism and if they did not delay in requesting Baptism from the Church, but was unable to receive the actual sacrament because of their untimely death. Baptism of blood is an occasion on which God might choose to offer someone baptismal grace without the sacrament of Baptism, if that person had unwavering faith and if they offered themselves and were killed out of others' hatred for faith in Christ.

4. Name three effects of Confirmation.

Three effects of Confirmation are completing the grace of our Baptism, raising us to spiritual maturity, and empowering us with mature spiritual responsibility. (Other possible answer: imprinting a new sacramental character on our souls.)

5. List the seven gifts of the Holy Spirit and the twelve fruits of the Holy Spirit.

The seven gifts are wisdom, understanding, counsel, strength, knowledge, and piety.

The twelve fruits are charity, joy, peace, patience, kindness, goodness, generosity, gentleness, faithfulness, modesty, self-control, and chastity.

6. What are the six basic parts of the Mass?

The six basic parts of the Mass are the Gathering, the Liturgy of the Word, the Offertory, the Anaphora (or Offering), Communion, and the Dismissal.

7. Who can and cannot receive Communion? Why?

Only those who are baptized, in a state of grace, and have prepared by fasting for one hour can receive Communion because these conditions reflect our unity with Jesus. Those who are not baptized or are not in a state of grace commit sacrilege if they take Communion.

8. Name and define each of the three "parts" of confession.

The three parts of Penance are contrition, confession, and satisfaction. Contrition is the "sorrow of the soul and detestation for the sin committed, together with the resolution not to sin again." Confession is the vocal disclosure of our sins to a priest in the sacrament of Penance and Reconciliation. Satisfaction is "making up for our sins," repairing our relationship with God, which we do through the penance we are assigned by the priest.

ANSWER KEY

9. What is the difference between perfect and imperfect contrition?

Perfect contrition is complete contrition. It is sorrow for sins that comes from the right motivation, the love of God, and the desire to confess our sins as soon as possible. Imperfect sin, or "attrition," is not completed by the love of God but rather the fear of God's punishment for sin instead.

10. What are the three different ways that men can be sacramentally ordained to participate in Jesus's priesthood? Name and define each.

Men can be sacramentally ordained to participate in Jesus's priesthood as bishops, presbyters, and deacons. Bishops, or the office of bishop, is the fulfillment of the apostolic office. Presbyters, or priests, sit in council with the bishops and assist them in teaching, sanctifying, and governing the Church. Deacons help priests in the fulfilment of their apostolic duties, particularly that of charitable service.